Y0-EMJ-946

picturing THE WALT DISNEY FAMILY MUSEUM

picturing THE WALT DISNEY FAMILY MUSEUM

photography by JIM SMITH text by RICHARD BENEFIELD with an introduction by DIANE DISNEY MILLER

One of the comments we most enjoy from our Museum visitors is that there's never enough time to see and appreciate the art, artifacts, film, and video that fill our beautiful galleries. After viewing the rich details of Jim Smith's photos, I'm pleased to say that they not only portray the artistic highlights of our ten interactive galleries, but often capture the fresh ideas and imagination that filled my father's life.

Although we ask visitors to refrain from photography in order to protect original documents and art in the Museum, we hope that the images in this book will provide a souvenir of quality. Our Founding Executive Director, Richard Benefield, has provided the text to explain these photos that represent The Walt Disney Family Museum in its first year.

Enjoy this visual tour of our Museum!

— Diane Disney Miller

The Walt Disney Family Museum is nestled on the western edge of the Main Post of the Presidio of San Francisco—the largest urban National Park in the United States. The Museum is housed in one of five identical barracks built by the U.S. Army in the 1890s, a group of buildings that is part of a National Landmark District. From the grounds of the Museum, visitors have one of the most spectacular views of the Golden Gate Bridge in the San Francisco Bay Area.

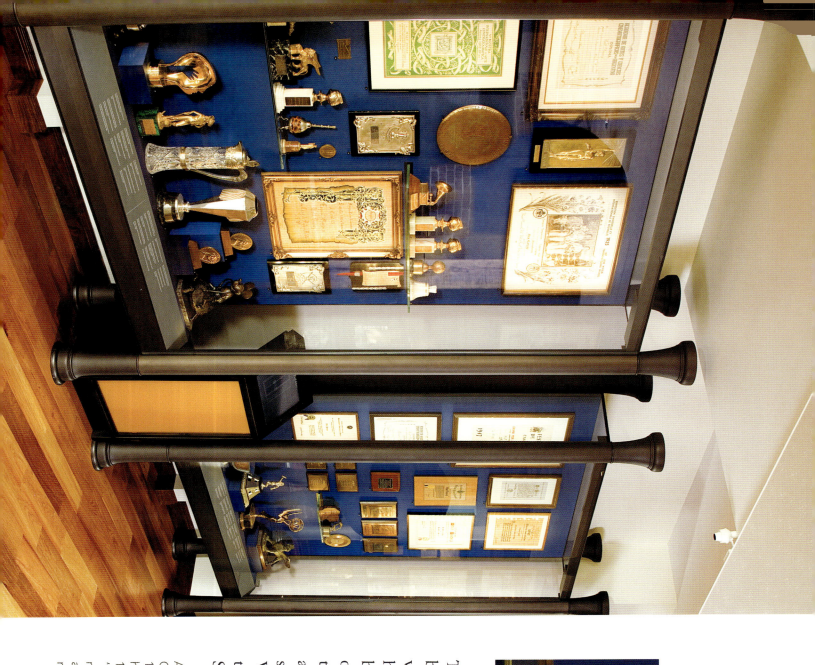

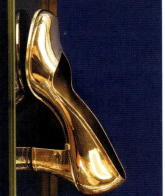

The staid exterior of the building belies the warm welcome that awaits visitors inside. Rich wood floors and historic building details provide the backdrop for state-of-the-art exhibits of a few of Walt Disney's more than 900 awards, interactive kiosks, and a tableau that incorporates some of the original furniture from Walt's personal apartment above the firehouse on Disneyland's Main Street, U.S.A.

Above: Silver slipper commemorating the Cinderella Contest held in conjunction with the 1953 release of the film in Japan. These contests had been held in the U.S. for the film's original 1950 release with publicity stating that the winner "must have character, personality, charm. It is not just beauty. It can be a cheerful disposition, a friendly helpful nature or a particular talent for making others happy."

Clockwise from top left: Key to the City of San Francisco presented to Walt in 1958; Presidential Medal of Freedom, 1964; Coast Guard "Oscar" for Men Against the Arctic, 1955; Trofeo d'Arte della Biennale—Snow White and the Seven Dwarfs—Seventh Venice Biennial International Festival of Motion Picture Art Award, 1938; and Emmy® Award presented to Walt, 1956, for Best Producer-Film Series, the Disneyland television show. Opposite: Furniture from Walt's Disneyland apartment.

Disneyland Apartment

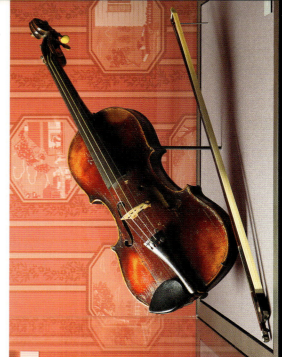

"The greatest wealth a man may acquire is the wisdom that he gains from living. And sometimes out of small beginnings, come the forces that shape a whole life."

John Tucker Battle, Screenwriter, *So Dear to My Heart*

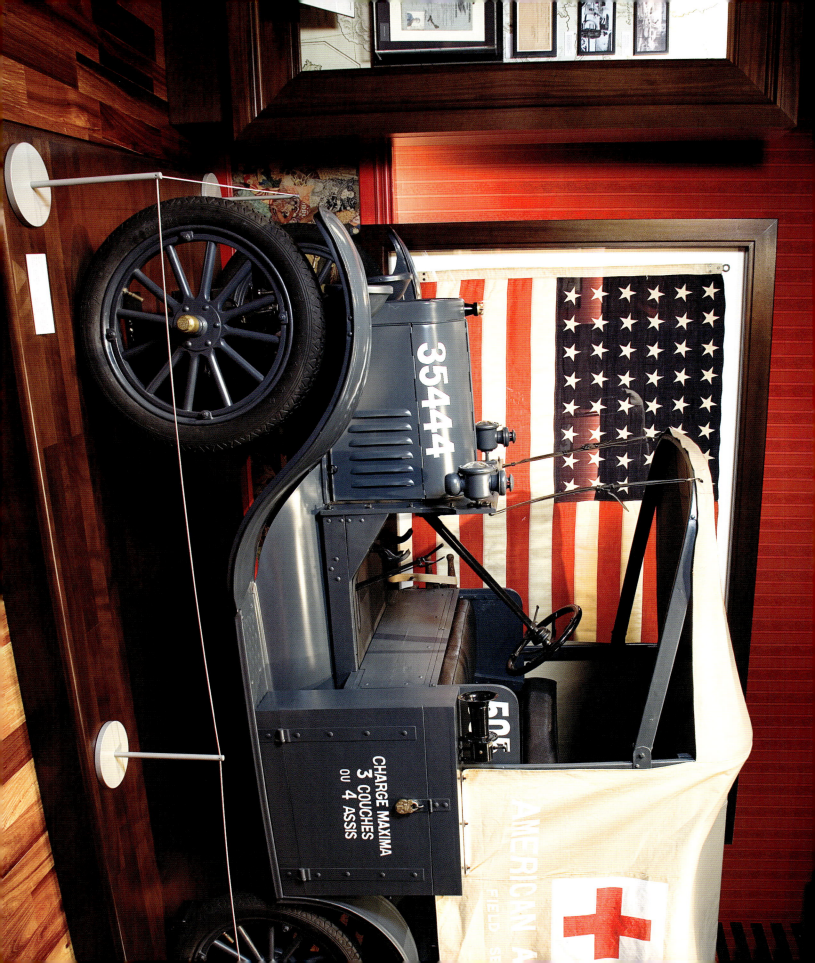

The first gallery in the Museum transports visitors back in time to the turn of the last century. Here the story is told of Walt's 1901 birth in Chicago and the family's subsequent moves to Marceline, Missouri; Kansas City; and back to Chicago. From an early age, Walt loved to draw, and a copy of his high school's magazine, *The Voice*, provides examples of his early artistic efforts. But the War was on, and Walt was restless to join up. Being too young for the military, he managed to sign up for the Red Cross. He arrived in France just as the War was ending and drove a Model T ambulance for almost a year before returning to the States.

Previous spread: Walt Disney at ten months. The fiddle that belonged to Walt's father, Elias. Left: Model T ambulance like the one Walt drove in France. Above: One of Walt's illustrations in *The Voice*.

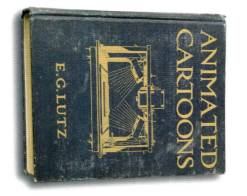

When Walt finished his tour of duty in France, Roy encouraged him to come to Kansas City and try his hand at becoming a commercial artist. While working for the Kansas City Film Ad Company, Walt met Ub Iwerks. The two learned animation from Lutz's book, and Walt was inspired to start his own company—Laugh-O-gram Films Inc. But the company failed, and Walt boarded a train for Hollywood, where he hoped to become a movie director.

"ROY SAID: 'LOOK, I THINK YOU SHOULD GET OUT OF THERE.'"

"THE DAY I GOT ON THAT SANTA FE, CALIFORNIA LTD, I WAS JUST FREE AND HAPPY. BUT I'D FAILED. I THINK IT'S IMPORTANT TO HAVE A GOOD HARD FAILURE WHEN YOU'RE YOUNG."

"The day I got on that Santa Fe, California Ltd. I was just free and happy. But I'd failed. I think it's important to have a good hard failure when you're young."

– Walt

An elevator decorated as a period railroad car delivers visitors to the upper floor galleries.

"I came to Hollywood and arrived here in August 1923 with forty dollars in my pocket and a coat and a pair of trousers that didn't match."

– Walt

Far right: Vintage cameras and filmmaking equipment are displayed throughout the Museum.

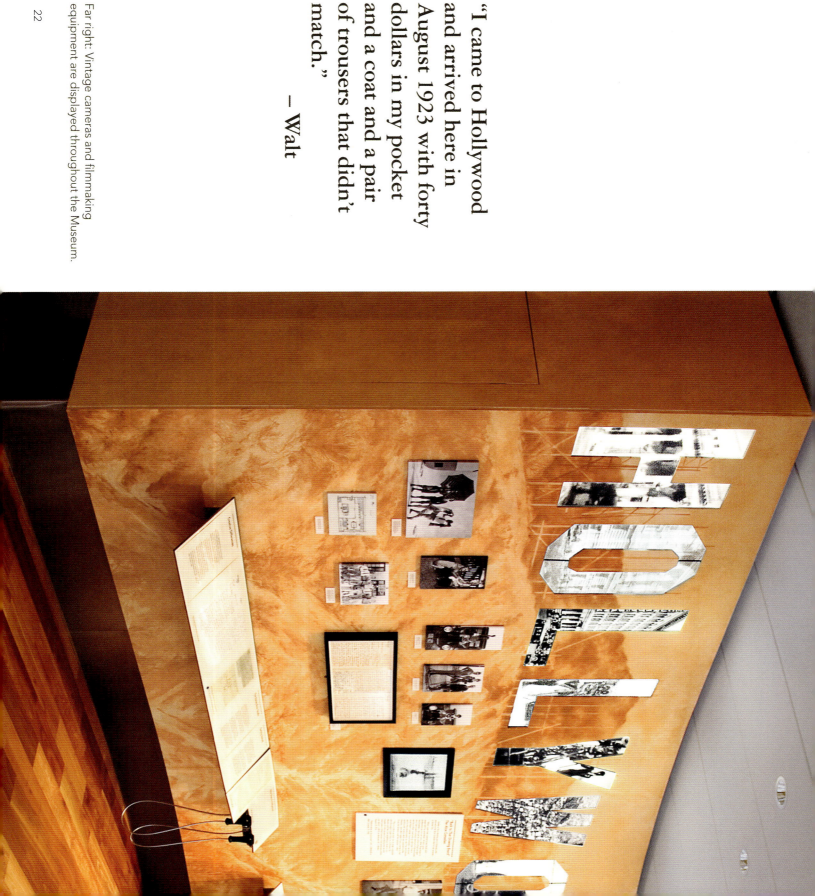

HOLLYWOOD

NOW PRESENTING

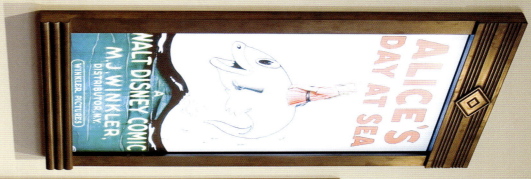

A
WALT DISNEY COMIC
M.J. WINKLER,
DISTRIBUTOR, N.Y.

WINKLER PICTURES

ALICE'S
DAY AT SEA

NOW SHOWING

ALICE
THE TOREADOR

by Walt
Disney

With a sample reel produced in Kansas City, Walt managed to sell the Alice Comedies. He immediately called for Ub to join him, and he also convinced the parents of young Virginia Davis to move to Hollywood. Virginia was the first of four little girls to play Alice in the series that combined live action with animation.

Above: Walt, second from left, directs Virginia Davis while Roy operates the camera.

W alt and Ub went on to create Oswald the Lucky Rabbit, a successful series of shorts that Walt lost to an unscrupulous distributor. Once Walt realized the rights to Oswald were no longer his, he set off in a new direction, declaring that he would never again lose control of his work. On a train ride from New York to Hollywood, Mickey, not Mortimer, Mouse was born out of a conversation between Walt and his wife, Lilly. Years later, the Disney family discovered among the business papers of one of Walt's companies, Retlaw, what is now considered the earliest known drawing of Mickey Mouse.

Above: Vintage Oswald poster. Opposite: The earliest known drawing of Mickey Mouse.

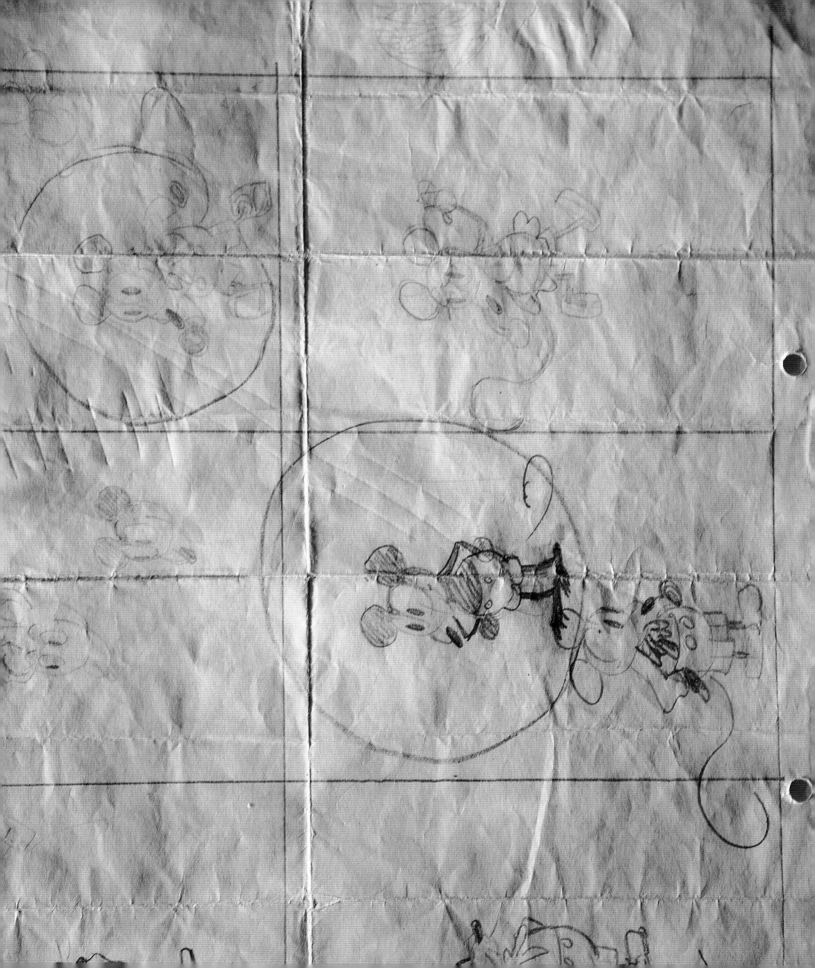

Animating Steamboat Willie

The art of the animator is to create the illusion of life. To create this illusion that a drawing can move—in effect, to give it the appearance of life. To create this illusion requires many drawings, each advancing the action slightly from the previous drawing. These 348 frame enlargements from *Steamboat Willie*, comprising less than one minute of action on the screen, demonstrate just how labor-intensive the craft of animation really was.

These drawings are primarily the work of Ub Iwerks, whose work on the early Disney cartoons was becoming well known both for its quality and for his prodigious output. Iwerks had previously animated the first Mickey Mouse picture, *Plane Crazy*, singlehandedly, and is said to have turned out as many as 700 drawings in one day—a figure that became legendary in the industry.

346 drawings from *Steamboat Willie*, which account for less than 15 seconds of film, pay tribute to artist Ub Iwerks, who drew the earliest Mickey cartoons. An interactive exhibit (opposite) allows visitors to try their hand at synching sound to film.

Mickey Mouse was an overnight sensation. Licensing of the mouse was a global success, and the Museum displays a robust collection of vintage Mickey merchandise.

Above: A group of vintage dolls and storybooks. Opposite: Clock, 1933; radio, 1934; and toy with bisque figures, 1930s.

"I only hope that we never lose sight of one thing—
that it was all started by a mouse."

—Walt

The Mickey Mouse shorts were popular and lucrative, but Walt ambitiously tackled a second series with a more flexible format, one that allowed him to experiment with music, depth, color, and character. The Silly Symphonies provided the laboratory for these experiments, produced animated shorts that have become classics, and honed the skills of his artists.

Above: Windup toys, 1930s.

"who's afraid of the big bad wolf?"

Three Little Pigs was a sensation at the box office and a breakthrough for Walt and his artists in the use of "personality animation"—the expression of a character's personality through the way the character moves.

Opposite: Popup book, Les Trois Petits Cochons, 1936.

Clockwise from above left: Character model of Goofy; character model of Pluto; and Mickey and Minnie toy piano, 1930s.

Distributed by RKO Radio Pictures, Inc.

HIS FIRST FULL LENGTH FEATURE PRODUCTION

Walt Disney's
Snow White
and the Seven Dwarfs
in the Marvelous
MULTIPLANE TECHNICOLOR

© W D P

Walt Disney's *Snow White and the Seven Dwarfs* was an enormous sensation. Reviews were rapturous, and Snow White and her seven dwarfs found their way into the hearts of moviegoers. It became a classic overnight.

Above: Concept painting by Gustav Tenggren.
Right: The first poster for the film.

Walt inscribed a copy of the Snow White book to his daughter, Diane Marie Disney.

Top left: Vintage storybook. Bottom left: Character model of Dopey. Opposite: An interactive exhibit challenges visitors to choose the correct music for a film clip.

For the premiere on December 21, 1937, Lilly Disney wore a *Snow White and the Seven Dwarfs* charm bracelet made by Cartier, and Walt may have had the money clip in his pocket that evening. The Museum has numerous pieces of personal memorabilia that aid in telling the story of Walt's family life.

An interactive wall pays tribute to the many collaborators who worked with Walt on *Snow White*.

An animator's desk comes to life with film clips from *Pinocchio*, the studio's next feature-length film. Character models, drawings, and documentary material complement the exhibit.

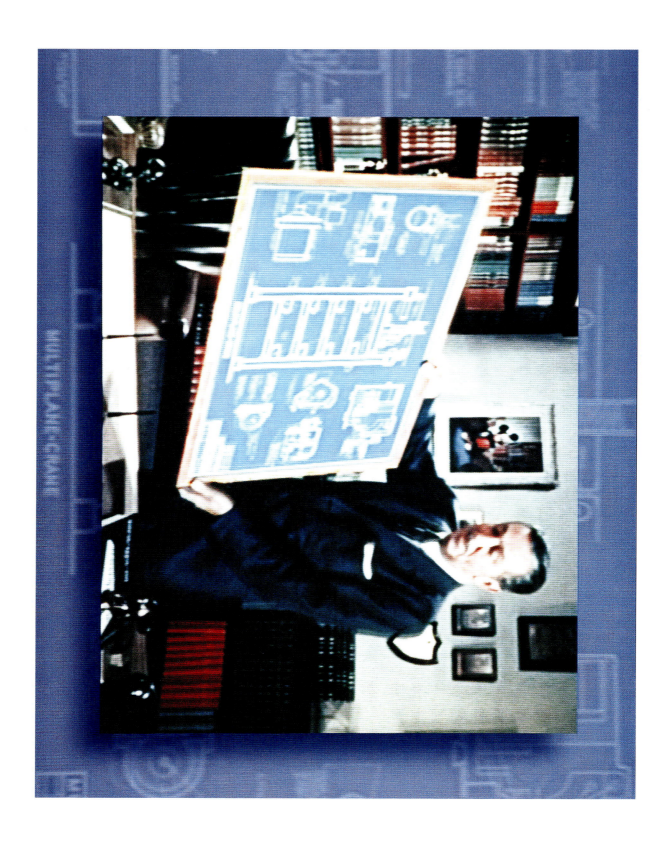

The multiplane camera was invented at the Walt Disney Studios to aid in achieving depth in animation. One of only three that were built is installed at The Walt Disney Family Museum. Walt explains how the multiplane camera works on a nearby video monitor and listening station.

"This is not the cartoon medium…. We have worlds to conquer here."

–Walt

Clockwise from top left: Ben Ali Gator character model; storyboard painting of Ben Ali Gator; and Hyacinth Hippo character model.

Fantasia was a tour-de-force in every sense of the word. Stories, characters, and, in some cases, abstract art were created to visualize great works of classical music. The largest video screen in the Museum lets visitors experience *Fantasia* and hear from some of those who collaborated on the film. Cases display original concept art for the film as well as materials documenting Walt's relationship with well-known artists, composers, and conductors of the day.

Above: *Fantasia* story drawing of Mickey as the Sorcerer's Apprentice. Left: A film still from "Ave Maria," *Fantasia's* finale, provides a dramatic gallery backdrop.

The most difficult time in Walt's life was the 1941 strike at the Studio. He subsequently appeared before the House Un-American Activities Committee. Both are represented in the Museum.

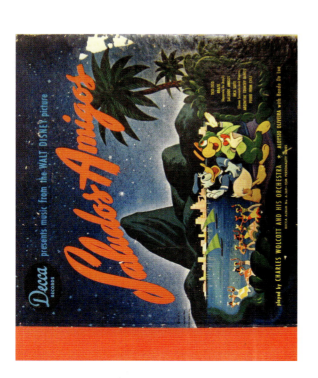

As the Studio strike was underway, Walt and a group of his artists, nicknamed El Grupo, embarked on a Good Neighbor tour through Latin America. As they were making friends of our neighbors, they absorbed the visual and musical culture that later infused the films, *Saludos Amigos* and *The Three Caballeros*.

Above: Vintage album cover. Right: Walt in the costume of a gaucho.

Once the strike was over, Walt finished *Dumbo*. When the U.S. entered World War II, the Studio diverted its resources in support of the war effort.

Far left: Casey Jr. character model.
Above: Vintage film poster.

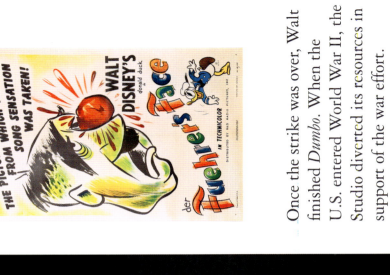

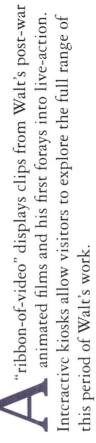

A "ribbon-of-video" displays clips from Walt's post-war animated films and his first forays into live-action. Interactive kiosks allow visitors to explore the full range of this period of Walt's work.

SEE PAGES 6, 7, AND 8 FOR RENEWAL,
EXTENSION, AMENDMENTS, LIMITATIONS,
AND RESTRICTIONS.

SEE PAGES 6, 7, AND 8 FOR RENEWAL,
EXTENSION, AMENDMENTS, LIMITATIONS,
AND RESTRICTIONS.

A bracelet of miniature Oscars®, which Walt gave to Lilly, reminds visitors that Walt was awarded more individual Academy Awards® than anyone else in history. Walt's wristwatch and home-movie camera as well as his and Lilly's passports are nearby.

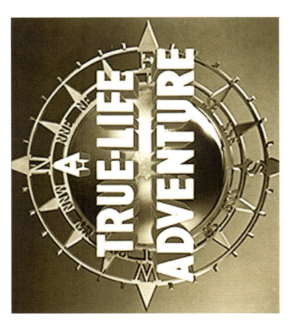

As visitors leave the 1890s barracks and move into the new glass-and-steel pavilion, they are afforded a spectacular view of San Francisco Bay and the Golden Gate Bridge. Video monitors showing clips of the True-Life Adventures and other documentaries are imbedded in the opposite wall.

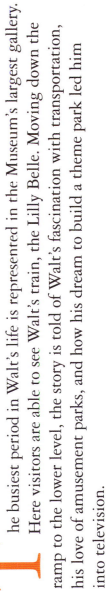

The busiest period in Walt's life is represented in the Museum's largest gallery. Here visitors are able to see Walt's train, the Lilly Belle. Moving down the ramp to the lower level, the story is told of Walt's fascination with transportation, his love of amusement parks, and how his dream to build a theme park led him into television.

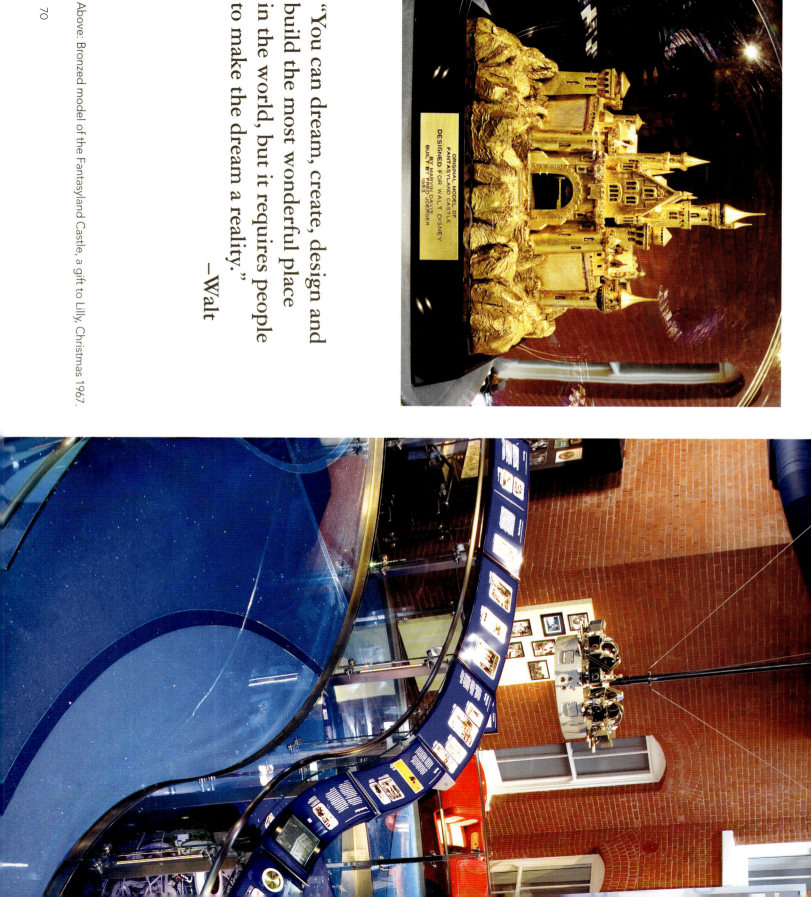

"You can dream, create, design and build the most wonderful place in the world, but it requires people to make the dream a reality."

—Walt

Above: Bronzed model of the Fantasyland Castle, a gift to Lilly, Christmas 1967.

"You can dream, create, design and build the most wonderful place in the world, but it requires people to make the dream a reality."

Main Street, U.S.A.

"I use the same talents to develop the different attractions at the park that I do to make my cartoons and make my other films here."

—Walt

An intricately-detailed model is an artistic interpretation of Disneyland as Walt might have imagined it.

Even as the Walt Disney Studio continued to produce animated and live-action films, Walt embraced the medium of television with programs like *Disneyland*, *Walt Disney Presents*, *Walt Disney's Wonderful World of Color*, and *The Mickey Mouse Club*.

Clockwise from left: Vintage ring, about 1955; miniature Atomobile used in the "Adventure Thru Inner Space" attraction at Disneyland; and a Davy Crockett coonskin cap and rifle.

Walt's diverse activities in the 1960s included work on the 1960 Winter Olympics in Squaw Valley, California, and the 1964-65 New York World's Fair. The Olympic Torch was designed at the Disney Studios.

FUN at the FAIR...

where and how to find it

Disneyland fun at the fair

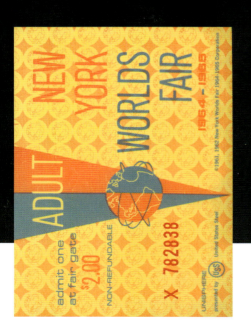

NEW YORK
WORLDS FAIR
1964 – 1965

ADULT

admit one
at fair gate $2.00
NON-REFUNDABLE

X 782838

UNISPHERE
presented by U.S. United States Steel

©1961, 1965 New York Worlds Fair 1964-1965 Corporation

© WED Enterprises, Inc. 1964

Pepsi-Cola presents
**Walt Disney's
'It's a Small World –
a Salute to UNICEF'
at the New York
World's Fair 1964–1965**

At the same time that Walt was scoring successes in television and theme parks, his motion-picture enterprise continued to thrive. Live-action films included *Old Yeller*, *Darby O'Gill and the Little People*, and *Pollyanna*. Among the memorable animated features were *Sleeping Beauty*, *101 Dalmatians*, and *The Sword in the Stone*. *Mary Poppins* combined live action with animation and became an instant classic. The Museum exhibits Walt's personal copy of P.L. Travers's book (above).

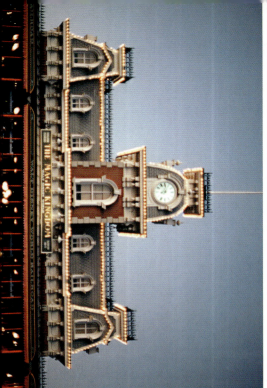

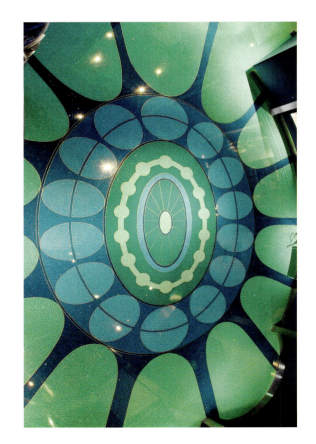

I n his last years, Walt was hard at work on his Experimental Prototype Community of Tomorrow (Epcot) and a theme park for Florida, which Roy, following Walt's death, would name Walt Disney World. The gallery floor design was inspired by a plan drawing for Epcot.

The world responded in shock and grief at Walt's untimely death in 1966 at age 65. Editorial cartoons from the time as well as telegrams of condolence sent to Lilly fill a gallery. Walt is captured (above) in a characteristic gesture, tipping his hat, on his last memorable family outing—a yacht trip out of Vancouver in July 1966.

In the final gallery of the Museum, visitors experience Walt's life and legacy in a video immersion while hearing a piano transcription of Beethoven's Pastoral Symphony.

Copyright © 2010 The Walt Disney Family Museum, LLC

Published by The Walt Disney Family Museum, LLC. No part of this book may be reproduced or transmitted in any form or by any means, electronic or mechanical, including photocopying, recording, or by any information storage and retrieval system, without written permission from the publisher.

All photographs, except as noted, copyright © 2010 Jim Smith. All Rights Reserved. Photographs pages 6, 15 (top right), 25, 50, 55 (right), 69, 80, and 83 courtesy The Walt Disney Company, © Disney Enterprises, Inc. Photographs pages 26, 39, 40 (top left), 42 (top left), 48 (right), 51, 55 (left), 57 (right), and 79 by Mark Gibson, © Walt Disney Family Foundation. Page 52 UCLA Film & Television Archive. Page 85 frame from home movie shot by and © Ron Miller.

First Edition
10 9 8 7 6 5 4 3 2 1
Reinforced binding
Library of Congress Cataloging in Publication Data on file
ISBN 978-0-615-39931-7

Book concept by Jim Smith
Design by Em Dash
Printed in China

Lilly Belle and Carolwood Pacific are trademarks and service marks of the Walt Disney Family Foundation. Walt Disney Family Museum, The Walt Disney Family Foundation, The Walt Disney Family Museum, Disneyland, EPCOT, Mickey Mouse, Silly Symphonies, Snow White, Pinocchio, Bambi, and Fantasia are trademarks of Disney Enterprises, Inc. The Academy Awards and Oscar are registered trademarks and service marks of the Academy of Motion Picture Arts and Sciences. The Emmy name and the Emmy statuette are the trademarked property of The Academy of Television Arts & Sciences and the National Academy of Television Arts & Sciences. All other trademarks referred to herein are the property of their respective owners. The Walt Disney Family Museum is not affiliated with The Walt Disney Company.

I walked into The Walt Disney Family Museum as a San Francisco tourist, and left having learned about a true American genius, Walt Disney. In fact, I felt like I met Walt Disney and he himself led me through the Museum. I left, not only with a great admiration for Walt and his family, but also the dream of creating a photo book that would capture the experience of visiting this most magical of places.

I could never thank enough the remarkable people who worked so hard to make this dream a reality. I wish to express my gratitude to my photo crew, Amelia Panico, Stephen Titra, and Mike Vasilauskas, and my colleagues, Constance Synder of CRSR Designs, Susan Chaires of Chaires and Associates, and my studio helpers, Mike Turek, Richard McGraw, Mike Bush and Judy Lieberman.

Thank you to all the incredible folks at the Museum: Marsha Robertson, Michael Labrie, Anel Muller, Laura Ellison, Jim Ventura, Katy Dashiell, and Richard Lorenzo. A special thanks to Lisa LaRue, who heard of my book and became its first fan. The entire staff of the Museum warmly welcomed me from the first moment of that first day, a thanks to each of you. I could never have made all the imaging happen without the wonderful and good humored help of John Stroh and Cassady Toles, who worked endless hours with me night after night in the Museum. So often, if there is magic in these photos, they helped make it happen.

It is also my good fortune to be collaborating with Em Dash, one of the most gifted design studios I have worked with. Each and every step of the way, Frank Kofsuske, Georgina Lee and Yolanda de Montijo, have made invaluable contributions to this project.

One of the best things about working on this book has been the opportunity to work with Richard Benefield. Richard has been what every book photographer dreams of finding, an incisive author as well as a magical champion of this book and all things Disney.

And I owe a debt to two families, the Walt Disney family, who have dedicated so much of their lives to keeping fresh and exciting the legacy of Walt Disney, and through this Museum continue to show to each and every visitor the wonders of a life lived with imagination.

And my family, Laura, Luke, Alison, and Matt, four wonderful Disney fans who often were my seven dwarfs.

And, thank you, Walt.

– Jim Smith